W9-BKS-824

FIRST-GLANCE FINANCE

# Starting a Business

Cavendish
Square
New York

Fran Hatton

Published in 2015 by Cavendish Square Publishing, LLC
243 5th Avenue, Suite 136, New York, NY 10016

Copyright © 2015 by Cavendish Square Publishing, LLC

First Edition

CPSIA Compliance Information: Batch #WW15CSQ

All websites were available and accurate when this book was sent to press.

Library of Congress Cataloging-in-Publication Data

Hatton, Fran.
Starting a business / Fran Hatton.
pages cm. — (First-glance finance)
Includes index.
ISBN 978-1-50260-104-9 (hardcover) ISBN 978-1-50260-108-7 (ebook)
1. New business enterprises. 2. Entrepreneurship. I. Title.

HD62.5.H374 2014
658.1'1—dc23

2014025528

Editor: Amy Hayes
Senior Copy Editor: Wendy A. Reynolds
Art Director: Jeffrey Talbot
Senior Designer: Amy Greenan
Senior Production Manager: Jennifer Ryder-Talbot
Production Editor: David McNamara
Photo Research by J8 Media

The photographs in this book are used by permission and through the courtesy of: Cover photos by
Arvind Balaraman/Moment Open/Shutterstock.com; Juan Camilo Bernal/Moment Open/Getty Images;
Arvind Balaraman/Shutterstock.com, 1; lendy16/Shutterstock.com, throughout; © North Wind Picture
Archives, 5; Corbis/Superstock, 7; © Look and Learn/Bridgeman Images, 8; Sergey Novikov/Shutterstock.
com, 10; John Lund/Marc Romanelli/Getty Images, 12; Niyazz/Shutterstock, 13; Vicky Kasala/Getty Images,
16; Lecic/Thinkstock, 19; Jupiterimages/Pixland/Thinkstock, 22; Maskot/Getty Images, 24; Exactostock/
Superstock, 26; Geri Lavrov/Getty Images, 27; altrendo images/Getty Images, 30; JGI/Jamie Grill/Getty
Images, 33; Carol Yepes/Getty Images, 36; Dori OConnell/Getty Images, 37; Xavier Bonghi/Getty Images, 38;
© iStockphoto.com/pkline, 39; Mikael Törnwall/Getty Images, 41.

Printed in the United States of America

# CONTENTS

ONE / 4

## First Businesses Through the Years

TWO / 9

## Why Run Your Own Business?

THREE / 15

## Making Your Business Work

FOUR / 23

## The Pros and Cons of Running Your Own Business

FIVE / 29

## The Best Way of Planning Your Business

SIX / 35

## Simple Businesses You Can Run

GLOSSARY / 42

FIND OUT MORE / 44

INDEX / 46

ABOUT THE AUTHOR / 48

# First Businesses Through the Years

·········································

One of the most common questions that people hear from a very young age is, "What do you want to be when you grow up?" As you consider your future, you might be thinking of a business in which you'd like to work. Maybe you have even wondered what it would be like to have your own business.

The earliest businesses were based on an agricultural society.

# The Early Days of Kids Working

After the Ice Age (12,000 BCE), early humans stopped roaming to hunt game and gather food to survive. People started settling down in groups to raise crops and domesticate animals. As towns and cities formed and connected with one another, words and numbers were needed to keep track of sales of property and **goods**. All ancient civilizations with a writing system had one message in common: people meant business.

One business often led to another. For example, farmers had to hire extra **labor** to help in the fields at harvest. Some clever person would set up a wagon to sell food and drink to the workers. Toolmakers made sure to have items in stock in case extra ploughs, hoes, or threshers were needed.

Individuals who now earned money could spend it. They became **consumers**, or people who buy products. At markets, shops, and bazaars in town, there were craftspeople and artisans selling everyday necessities, as well as luxuries such as jewelry. These markets weren't the only way of selling or buying items, either. Tradespeople hired agents who journeyed by caravan so that they could reach a bigger **market**. These agents were the first traveling salesmen.

Children performed a lot of jobs in these early societies. They tended to animals in herds. They learned to help make bricks and pottery, as well as weave, sew, and dye cloth. They could also help in the marketplace, run errands, and deliver messages. Kids could do these tasks, of course, because schools were mostly for the wealthy.

## Business Basics for All Ages

*Pleasure in the job puts perfection in the work.*
—Aristotle (384–322 BCE)

If a child today wants to work, the time spent working has to be balanced with the demands of school. Starting a business is a great way to set your own hours. You can spend as much time as your schedule allows, and scale back if needed.

No matter what, choose a business you enjoy and be committed to it. Having your own business is rewarding in many ways, and not just in the money you earn.

Whether you start with a brother, sister, or cousin, babysitting and childcare are services always in high demand.

**First Businesses Through the Years** 7

# The Hammurabi Code

**H**ammurabi was a great **Babylonian** king. He wanted to keep order in his expanding kingdom, so he began making a list of 282 laws, which were carved into a stone pillar.

Hammurabi realized there needed to be laws to govern business matters. He set standards for how payment must be made. Cash was the system most often used for buying and selling, but the king also decreed that people could still pay in produce or crops. Both payment systems had set values, or scales.

For example, Law 275 outlined the rate of pay, in *gerahs*, one form of money in the area, for skilled artisans. A potter received five gerahs for his work, a tailor five gerahs for his, a rope maker four gerahs, and so on. A mason would earn a set number of gerahs per each day of work.

# CHAPTER TWO

# Why Run Your Own Business?

**M**aking money is a great reason to run your own business. After all, there are probably many things you'd like to buy or activities you'd like to do, and most of them have a price. Compared with working for someone else, however, the advantage of owning your own business is that you get to be in charge. As the boss, you'll decide when to work, how much to work, and what you'll work on. It's very appealing, especially if you'd rather come up with

Accept the responsibilities for the job you have so you can enjoy the work you do.

ideas than follow directions. If the business does well, you get most of the **profit**. It can also be risky, however. If a business does poorly, the time and money you've invested in it is lost.

To start and run your own business, you don't have to come up with a brand-new idea. If you think of something that's never been done, great! However, tried-and-true jobs such as babysitting, pet sitting, yard work, and making crafts are always needed.

# High-End Hair Ties

If you visit the Emi-Jay website (*emi-jay.com*), you'll find a professional site that sells unique hair ties. What might surprise you is that two teenage **entrepreneurs**, Emily and Julianne, created this successful business when they were both in eighth grade! Your business may not become a success at the level of Emi-Jay, but anything's possible if you're prepared to work hard.

## Before Setting Up Shop

Before you decide what type of business you want to create, you really need to make sure you're doing it for the right reasons. You're going to have to work hard to be successful, so you should consider some of the following factors that go into starting your own business.

### Learning to Support Yourself

You can save up money that's been given to you, but how often do people just give you money? If you're really looking to be self-sufficient, you need to earn your own money. It is universally accepted wisdom that people

Purchases can be necessities or luxuries, items you need, or gifts for someone special.

think and act more cautiously and responsibly with funds they earned for themselves.

Now is a great time to learn what things cost, and not just the fun stuff like video games, trendy fashions, and candy. The term "cost of living" refers to how much money is needed to pay for everyday necessities. Talk to your parents about rent and mortgage payments, grocery and utility bills, and other basics. Even if you don't have to contribute to them yet, being knowledgeable about these cost of living **expenses** will give you a sense of scale.

# Do You Have to Pay Taxes?

**I**n the United States, the government needs money to pay for roads, parks, police, and more. It relies on all American citizens who are working and earning money to contribute a portion of it toward these necessary expenses by filing special forms with the Internal Revenue Service (IRS). Different filing rules apply to children, and even if you earn a small amount of income, you may be required to file under certain circumstances. Make sure to ask your parents or guardian for help. To learn more about taxes and small business, visit the IRS website, irs.gov.

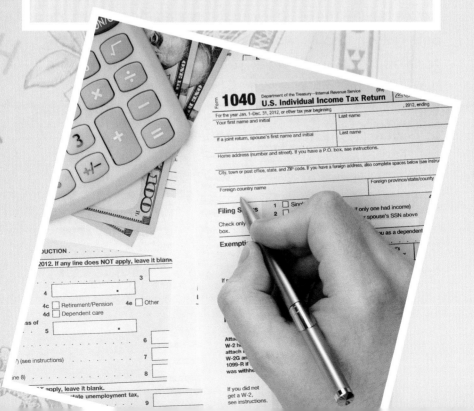

## Finding a Need and Selling to It

"You could sell a cup of water to a drowning man" is a witty compliment often given to a good entrepreneur. It's a clever turn of phrase because the opposite is usually true. It is extremely difficult to try to succeed in launching a new business, no matter how much heart or sweat you put into it. Take whatever idea you have and run it past your parents or another adult, such as a teacher. They can tell you if your plans are on the right track, or may be able to warn you about problems you might run into.

# Getting More Than Money

When the Beatles sang the lyrics, "money can't buy me love," they were right about a lot of things. Earning an income, especially when it's from your own business, makes buying things for yourself easier. Money isn't the only reason people work, though. It's also about feeling good about yourself when you can provide something that other people want, or help them finish a big task. You'll get a feeling inside that comes from accomplishing something, not just earning money.

# CHAPTER THREE

# Making Your Business Work

· · · · · · · · · · · · · · · · · · · · · · · · · · · · · · · · · · · · · · · · · ·

Once you know that you want to run your own business, you need to make sure you can actually make money. It would make no sense to do all that work, only to find that you're spending more than you actually earn. However, if you plan ahead, consider the costs of what you're doing, and stick to your plan, you will make a profit and discover what success feels like.

Planning ahead and thinking about initial costs is an important part of making your business a success.

# Raw Materials

Most businesses have **initial costs**, or expenses you must **incur** before you start to make any money. If you shovel driveways, for example, the initial cost would be incurred by buying your shovel. When you advertise with handmade flyers, the paper and markers you use are business costs, or **investments**. If you are making something to sell, such as a craft or lemonade, you will incur the cost of the raw materials needed to make your product.

Consider the last example, making lemonade. Kids run most lemonade stands using lemonade mix or homemade ingredients borrowed from their parents' kitchens. While that leads to pure profit, it's not a realistic model. If you want to build a long-term business, you need to consider what the ingredients cost, and not rely on using borrowed or donated ones.

Let's say that your recipe calls for five cups of sugar, twenty-five lemons, and a pitcher of water. If there are ten cups in a bag of sugar, you would be using about half of that

# Buying in Bulk

I f you make more of a single product, you can sometimes save money buying a lot of a certain ingredient at once. For example, a can of soda may be $1 at the store, but a twelve-pack might cost $3. In the twelve-pack, you are paying $.25 a can ($3 ÷ 12), which is much cheaper than $1 a can. You might be able to buy your raw materials in larger groups as well. Stores such as warehouse clubs sell groceries in larger quantities, so perhaps you can get a twenty-pound bag of sugar for $10, instead of buying four five-pound bags for $3 each, which would total $12. However, you need to be committed to your business, because any ingredients you buy but do not sell as product will reduce your profit.

to make the lemonade. If a bag of sugar costs $3.00, then the cost of lemonade is half of that.

$$\$3.00 \times \frac{1}{2} = \$1.50$$

Now, assume that five lemons are on sale for $2.00. If you need twenty-five lemons, how much will you pay for the lemons you need?

number of lemons in grouping → 

$$5\overline{)25}$$

number of groupings of lemons needed

number of lemons needed

5

-25

0

You will need five groupings of the lemons on sale. How much money will that be?

$$
\begin{array}{r}
5 \\
\times\ \$2.00 \\
\hline
\$10.00
\end{array}
$$

You'd need $10.00 worth of lemons, because twenty-five divided by five is five, and five times $2.00 (the cost of five lemons) is $10.00. You've now spent $1.50 for sugar and $10.00 for lemons, which adds up to $11.50.

The water is free in this example, so you've got all your costs figured, right? What about the cups that you serve your lemonade in? You may be able to use a pitcher from home, but your customers are going to want to leave with their lemonade, so you probably can't use your family's cups and glasses. If you assume paper cups are five cents each, and you need thirty cups for your lemonade, how much would you pay for cups?

$$\begin{array}{r}
\$.05 \\
\times\phantom{..}30 \\
\hline
\$1.50
\end{array}$$

Your cup cost would be $1.50, or thirty times five cents. Your cost of raw goods is now:

$$\begin{array}{l}
\$1.50 \text{ sugar} \\
\$10.00 \text{ lemons} \\
+\ \ \underline{\$1.50 \text{ cups}} \\
\phantom{+}\$13.00 \text{ raw goods}
\end{array}$$

Parts of your product can show that it's special, try to make it stand out.

# Pricing Your Product

Now that you've got your lemonade to sell, what will you charge per cup? The table below lists four options:

| Price per Cup | Cups Sold | Money Made | Cost to Make | Profit |
|---|---|---|---|---|
| $0.25 | 30 | $7.50 | $13.00 | -$6.50 |
| $0.50 | 30 | $15.00 | $13.00 | $2.00 |
| $0.75 | 30 | $22.50 | $13.00 | $9.50 |
| $1.00 | 30 | $30.00 | $13.00 | $17.00 |

In each of these options, the number of "Cups Sold" and amount of "Cost to Make" stay the same. However, the amount of money you make from those cups of lemonade change based on how much you charge. The first price, $0.25 a cup, is too low—you don't even make enough to pay for the ingredients! Some might think the second price, $0.50 a cup, is good enough. After all, you make $2. However, isn't your time worth something? If it took you an hour to make the lemonade and another hour to sell the lemonade, you would have spent two hours making $2. Is your time only worth $1 an hour?

In the third price example, you've made $9.50 after you've sold all your lemonade, and that seems better. Of course the fourth price, $1 a cup, makes the most profit, but you have to be careful not to overprice your product, or people will not buy it.

## Where to Go Next

Let's say you did sell your 30 cups of lemonade for $1 each, and you now have $30 in hand. If you are serious about running a business, you need to take some of that money and reinvest it, buying more ingredients for your next batch of lemonade. You can repeat everything you just did to sell another 30 cups the next day, or you can try some different things to grow your business.

If you're looking to grow, you could try to sell more of your product. Perhaps you turned away people because you ran out of lemonade, or some of your customers promised to tell their friends about your lemonade. Maybe you think you can sell 60 cups a day instead of 30. If you decide to do that, you will need to make twice as much lemonade, so you need twice the ingredients. If it cost $13 to make 30 cups, how much will it cost to make 60?

$$\begin{array}{r} 2 \\ \times\ \$13.00 \\ \hline \$26.00 \end{array}$$

Create something enjoyable, so it doesn't seem like work.

You are doubling everything, so the cost doubles as well. It will now cost $26.

Another way to grow a business is to offer more products. Perhaps you and your parents could come up with a second recipe, one for strawberry lemonade. You would want to test the recipe before you sell it, in order to ensure you have a good product that people want. Businesses call this process of inventing new products research and development.

# CHAPTER FOUR

# The Pros and Cons of Running Your Own Business

. . . . . . . . . . . . . . . . . . . . . . . . . . . . . . . . . . . . . . . . . . . . . . . . . . . .

**E**ven if you have a great idea for a business, you still need to decide whether or not you want to make that business a reality. Consider making a list of the positives and negatives of running your own business before you get started.

Make sure to list out the pros and cons of your business. Having a business with friends could be a great pro!

Sometimes an idea can be listed on both sides—you may think that making money is a positive, but if you need to invest money in your business and you are not successful, you may lose money, clearly a negative. Being your own boss can be a positive, but not having a boss that can teach you the basics of the work can be a negative as well. You really need to think hard about whether you should start down your entrepreneurial path. You can learn many useful lessons as you move forward. Here are some common things to consider.

## Do You Have the Time to Make Your Business Work?

Adults talk about time management all the time. It's a simple concept, and one that will be important to you the rest of your life. Basically, time management means you think of all the things you are supposed to be doing and make sure they get done.

Time management becomes important once you decide to start a business. If you start a lawn mowing business, you need to figure out how many lawns you can mow in an hour. If you know that it takes thirty minutes to mow most customers' yards, then you can start scheduling your services. Make sure to plan for extra time as well. You shouldn't try to mow two yards in one hour. After all, you might need to add in time to move your equipment to the next house or to talk to your customers.

Constantly reevaluate your time. You may under-commit or over-commit at first. It may involve some stumbles to get to where you want to be, but eventually you'll adapt, learn, and make progress. Don't worry. Many entrepreneurs say that it takes a lot of wrong turns to get to the right place.

## Balancing Your Business with School and Fun

Once you know how much time you can commit to your business, you might be tempted to do it as often as possible. If you can earn $10 by shoveling one walkway, then why not earn $40 shoveling four? There are a number of reasons to not overdo it, but the biggest is that you don't want to burn yourself out.

Working and earning money is great, but life is full of priorities. Even the best business people have days off.

Adults have to balance work and family every day. Talk over ideas or concerns you have with parents or other adults you trust.

Adults have priorities like taking care of families, running errands, and housework. Kids have priorities, too. Even if your business is going great, remember that school must be a priority. Homework, family time, chores, and more must be considered as you think about how much time you will put into your business.

In addition, give yourself time to have a little fun with your friends. While it is important to keep any commitments you make, you don't want to miss out on

# Planning for the Job You Don't Even Know You'll Have

**S**ome of the best benefits of running your own business don't come until later in life. You may not realize it, but when you run your own business, you are learning skills that you may apply in the future, both at work, in school, or even your family and social life. Planning how to buy the ingredients for your lemonade stand is known as budgeting, and it's something you'll be doing for the rest of your life. You'll just have a head start on how to best do it.

something fun because you chose to give all your time to your business. With all of this in mind, it's fair to say that the time you spend working can often be considered a pro and a con.

Being your own boss can also end up being both a positive and a negative. If a fun activity with your friends comes up, you can decide you want to adjust your schedule to make time to do it. However, this might not work if you've selected a business that has a specific schedule, like a paper route or a dog walking business. In those cases, if you don't do the work, customers will not be satisfied.

## Saving and Investing the Money You Make

Making money is something that will almost always end up in the "pro" column. Once you start earning a profit, you also have to decide what to do with it. Some kids spend money as fast as they get it on things such as movies, pizzas, and books. However, taking your profit and saving it over time will give you the ability to buy a more expensive item, like a video game or a bike. Putting your profits in the bank might help you be ready to buy something down the line that isn't even available yet!

Once you've put some thought into your reasons for starting your own business, you've hopefully come to the conclusion that the idea is worth pursuing.

# CHAPTER FIVE

# The Best Way of Planning Your Business

................................................................

Once you decide that you're going start your own business, you need to take the steps necessary to get things up and running. The more prepared you are, the more confident you will feel about your business, and the higher the likelihood it will be a success. Things will never be perfect. Problems will come up that you are not ready to handle, but planning ahead will minimize possible issues.

Tools of the trade can vary in cost so you need to work with what gets the job done best at an affordable price.

# Obtaining the Supplies You Need

For any business you choose, you will need supplies to do your job. The supplies come in two categories. The tools and hardware of a business are **durable goods**. Your shovel for snow removal or your computer for selling products online most likely will not have to be replaced very often. However, supplies such as rock salt to melt the ice, or the stamps, boxes, and packing materials for shipping your products are **consumable**, which means they get used up and need to be replenished. Unless you already have your durable goods, they will be an expense you need to absorb early. Your consumables will be a constant expense that you must pay for over time. These costs must be factored into your business plan, and you must constantly check your supply levels in order to make sure you've got what you need to meet your commitments.

When you're launching your business, you need to balance your need for supplies with the flexibility of being able to look around and search for bargains. Also, you only want to buy supplies that you will be using. Don't overbuy until your client base is built up and you understand what you'll use during the average week or month.

## Setting Up for Your Big Debut

Creating checklists is important at several stages of doing business. Make sure you plan ahead for doing the job over a period of time, such as several days of lemonade sales, or two weekends of babysitting or pet sitting. It's always better to start slow and then add more customers or products, because it is much easier than having to cut back. If you are filling orders for a product, such as making gift baskets, be sure to figure in the time it takes to finish creating each one, as well as the time it takes for delivery or being available if the product is to be picked up.

You will make mistakes, even with the best planning and equipment. If you learn from what went wrong, you can make your business better. If you have a run-in with some other dogs the first time you use a specific route in your dog walking business, you'll learn not to take that path again. You adapt and grow when you really look at why something didn't work successfully.

## Getting the Word Out About Your Business

Even the best business won't be successful if nobody knows about it. You need to get out and advertise and market your business. You can choose from different

# Minimum Wage
# State to State

States where the cost of living is higher, such as California and Connecticut, have higher minimum wages, or base rates than most other states. For instance, you could be earning $8.50 an hour in one state doing a job in a national retail chain or working at a fast-food restaurant, but if you were to relocate to another state, there might be a change in pay.

types of **marketing** depending on the type of business you are running, including word of mouth, flyers, advertisements, and a website.

## Word of Mouth

Most of your first customers will be your friends and family, and telling them about your business, or word of mouth, is the simplest form of promoting it. However, word of mouth doesn't just come from you telling people you know about your business. Word of mouth is also effective when one of your customers tells their friends and family about your business. For example, if the family you babysit for tells their neighbor who just had a baby about the wonderful job you're doing

A business exchange where both parties walk away happy is a success.

for them, you now have a shot at a new customer. Your chances of expanding your business will improve with great recommendations from your current customers.

## Flyers

If you're looking for ways to get your business's name out to more people, creating a flyer that tells customers what you can do is another great way to get your information out there. Strike a balance between catching people's eyes and giving them the information they need. If you have any specific qualifications or certifications, be sure to list them on your flyer. If you passed a babysitting certification class, that information should be on your flyer so parents will know you have training that will come in handy if you are watching their children. Once you've created your flyer, have a parent or friend look it over. You are starting a business and want to make

# Staying Safe

**W**hile you need to provide contact information to market your business, you need to be very careful when dealing with strangers, so work with your parents or guardian to decide how potential customers should contact you: via email, for example, or your family's phone number. Always have one of them or another responsible adult come with you when you first meet any new customers.

sure your business looks professional. Make copies of your flyer and post them in local coffee shops, stores, or community bulletin boards.

## On the Internet

If your business is getting bigger, or you are doing a mail-order business, you may need to create a website for your business. Once again, this is something you need to do with the help of a parent or guardian. Seek out websites for similar businesses to give yourself ideas for an effective website for your business.

# CHAPTER SIX

# Simple Businesses You Can Run

You've decided that you're ready to commit to running your own business. You've weighed the pros and cons, and are ready to do all the preparation you need, so what business should you pick? Businesses you want to consider fall into the following categories: labor, manufacture, and service. Each choice has its own demands and benefits. It's up to you to weigh the good with the bad. How much time do you have to give to your business? What extra tools or items will you need to purchase? Are there any certificates or permissions required?

Seasonal work means you have to be ready to take on what nature delivers.

## Labor Jobs

You have probably helped your family around the house for years already, and if you're willing to do the work, people always need an extra hand in and out of the house. For example, there are always outdoor chores to do, including weeding and mowing in spring and summer, raking leaves in the fall, and shoveling snow in the winter. These jobs require physical strength and protective wear such as gloves and boots. You could start out small doing basic yard chores in the spring and summer. Look into getting your own

Handle the products you sell with care.

rake and supply of lawn and leaf bags and head through your neighborhood to see who wants to hire you.

You don't have to limit chore work to the outdoor activities. People need help cleaning and organizing their houses, apartments, garages, and more. You can also run errands for customers, taking their packages to be mailed or doing simple shopping.

# Manufacturing Jobs

## Making Crafts

You've probably been making crafts since preschool. Look around and think about a craft that people would be willing to buy. You might want to consider how to sell the items you love constructing. This kind of business not only requires your time and talent, but also materials with which to build your products.

No matter what you are selling, it is a good idea to think about how you package it. Take care to keep the item safe for transport and delivery, but also have fun making the boxes or wrapping attractive. One touch of

A simple storefront for your business displays what you sell, and you can decorate to attract attention.

smart packaging is including your name or business name and contact information printed in some form.

## Selling Lemonade

It seems like a cliché, but selling lemonade is a solid choice for a warm-weather business. You can **diversify** the tried-and-true menu with a variety of choices, whether it's sugar-free lemonade, a berry-mixed version, or iced tea. These options, alongside the classic summertime beverage, will not only satisfy your customers but will most likely make them remember your stand. You can also try out different areas in your neighborhood or town that make a sensible place for the lemonade stand. If you have limited supplies and few

# Business
# Cards

Y ou're never too young to have a business card. Business cards originate from the calling card from the past. This was a simple card with one's name printed on it, which was presented to announce a visit or acknowledge a business or social introduction.

This is advertising in its simplest form. The business card is an inexpensive way to stand out for service jobs. There are software programs to help you, and you can get as creative as you'd like. Think of colors to use, and choose from the many different fonts, or styles of typeface, that are easily available in any word processing program.

helpers, staying close to your house is essential because you'll need to replenish your stores and don't want to have to drag your table, chair, sign, and products a long way. There is much to be said about location, however, and if there is a particular corner or street that gets more traffic and customers, then that's where you want to be.

## Service Jobs

Babysitting is a classic example of a service job. It is traditionally a starter job for girls, but more and more, boys can take advantage of the opportunities as well. You may want to get certified in order to best represent yourself to parents.

Pet ownership in the United States is higher today than it has ever been. Estimates vary, but roughly stated there are 75 million or more pet dogs and 84 million house cats. Add in the 17 million birds and countless aquarium fish and reptiles, and there's a good chance you can have a pet care business up and running in no time.

## Starting Your Business Adventure

Now that you have all this information on how to start a business, your job is to get it going. There are two main principles to keep in mind. The first is that your work is to be a point of pride, because it's a reflection of you. The second is that earning your own money gives you a sense of what it takes to support yourself, and saving it provides for your future.

Walking dogs can be a fun way to earn money and get some fresh air.

Are you ready to get started? Steer your plans and actions in the right direction for your first business. Don't be afraid of making some mistakes, because you will learn from everything you try. Remember that asking advice of your parents, teachers, and even business professionals is a great way to continue expanding your knowledge and opportunities. Starting and building your own business brings endless possibilities, and success will be yours in no time at all.

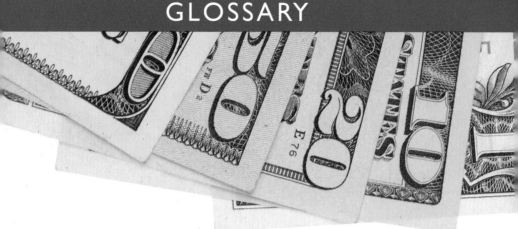

**Babylonian** Part of the ancient civilization of Babylon, in Mesopotamia.

**consumable** A product that is intended to be used up relatively quickly.

**consumer** The individual who purchases goods and services of a business.

**diversify** To increase the variety of products.

**durable goods** Supplies that, once purchased, may not need to be replaced.

**entrepreneur** An individual who starts his or her own business.

**expense** Something on which money is spent.

**goods** Physical items or products that are used in manufactures or are intended for sale.

**incur** To bring upon, as in debt or money owed.

**initial costs** The money and time needed to set up a business.

**investment** Use of money and resources to run a business for profit.

**labor** Workers; also refers to jobs that deal with physical or mental effort.

**manufacture** Deals with making goods for sale.

**market** The relationship of a business to consumers.

**marketing** The act of promoting and informing people of a product or service.

**profit** The amount left over after the cost of doing business is subtracted.

**service** An action provided for sale.

**supply** Amount of a good or service that producers will provide at given prices and at a given time.

**value** An estimate of an asset's worth.

## Books

Bernstein, Daryl. *Better Than a Lemonade Stand!: Small Business Ideas for Kids*. New York, NY: Aladdin/Beyond Words, 2012.

Rankin, Kenrya. *Start It Up: The Complete Teen Business Guide to Turning Your Passions Into Pay*. San Francisco, CA: Zest Books, 2011.

Toren, Adam, and Matthew Toren. *Kidpreneurs: Young Entrepreneurs With Big Ideas!* Phoenix, AZ: Business Plus Media Group, 2009.

# Websites

## Biz Kids

bizkids.com

Find out about kid entrepreneurs just like you! Watch the show, read the blog, and play games that will help you find out what it takes to create a successful business.

## E-How's Starting a Business As a Teenager

www.ehow.com/how_2066227_start-business-as-teenager.html

This article provides a simple, step-by-step guide on how to create a business.

## Youth Entrepreneurship

www.sba.gov/content/youth-entrepreneurship

This area of the Small Business Association's site provides a wealth of information for teenagers looking to start, manage, or grow a business.

Page numbers in **boldface** are illustrations.

advertise, 16, 31
    business card, 39
    flyer, 16, 32–34
    website, 32, 34
    word of mouth, 32

Babylonian, 7
business costs, 16
business types
    babysitting, 7, 10,
       31–33, 40
    crafts, 10, 16, 37
    dog walking, 28, 31, **41**
    labor, 36–37
    lemonade, 16–20, 22, 27,
       31, 38

manufacture, 37–38, 40
    organizing garages, 37
    organizing houses, 37
    pet sitting, 10, 31
    raking leaves, 36
    service, 40
    weeding and mowing, 36
    yard chores, 36

consumable, 30
consumer, 6
cost of living, 12, 32

diversify, 38
durable goods, 30

email, 34
entrepreneur, 11, 14, 24–25
expense, 12–13, 16, 30

gerahs, 8
goods, 5, 19

Hammurabi Code, 8

incur, 16
initial costs, 16, **16**
Internal Revenue Service
   (IRS), 13
investment, 16

labor, 5, 35

manufacture, 35
market, 6
marketing, 32, 34

profit, 10, 15–17, 20–21, 28

reinvest, 21
research and development,
   22
risk, 10

service, 7, 25, 35, 39
smart packaging, 38
starting a business
   budgeting, 27
   creating checklists, 31
   first customers, 32
   pros and cons, 23–24, 28
   setting priorities, 26
   supplies, 30–31, 38
   time management, 24–25
staying safe, 34
storefront, **38**
supply, 30, 37

**Fran Hatton** is a freelance author and editor who has spent her entire career working with the printed word in one form or another. She has written several books for Cavendish Square, including another in the First-Glance Finance series, *Learning About Earning*. Her husband and children bring her more joy than all the books in the world, and nothing can compete with that. A native of Indiana, Ms. Hatton now resides in Orlando, Florida.